T E R A T O L O G Y

The Lexi Rudnitsky First Book Prize in Poetry is a collaboration between Persea Books and The Lexi Rudnitsky Poetry Project. It sponsors the annual publication of a collection by an American woman who has yet to publish a full-length poetry book.

Lexi Rudnitsky (1972–2005) grew up outside of Boston. She studied at Brown University and Columbia University, where she wrote poetry and cultivated a profound relationship with a lineage of women poets that extends from Muriel Rukeyser to Heather McHugh. Her own poems exhibit both a playful love of language and a fierce conscience. Her writing appeared in *The Antioch Review, Columbia: A Journal of Literature and Art, The Nation, The New Yorker, The Paris Review, Pequod,* and *The Western Humanities Review.* In 2004, she won the Milton Kessler Memorial Prize for Poetry from Harpur Palate. Lexi died suddenly in 2005, just months after the birth of her first child and the acceptance for publication of her first book of poems, *A Doorless Knocking into Night* (Mid-List Press, 2006). The Lexi Rudnitsky First Book Prize in Poetry was founded to memorialize her and to promote the type of poet and poetry in which she so spiritedly believed.

Previous winners of the Lexi Rudnitsky First Book Prize in Poetry:

2013   Leslie Shinn, *Inside Spiders*
2012   Allison Seay, *To See the Queen*
2011   Laura Cronk, *Having Been an Accomplice*
2010   Cynthia Marie Hoffman, *Sightseer*
2009   Alexandra Teague, *Mortal Geography*
2008   Tara Bray, *Mistaken for Song*
2007   Anne Shaw, *Undertow*
2006   Alena Hairston, *The Logan Topographies*

TERATOLOGY

POEMS

SUSANNAH NEVISON

WINNER OF THE LEXI RUDNITSKY FIRST BOOK PRIZE

A Karen & Michael Braziller Book
PERSEA BOOKS / NEW YORK

Persea Books, Inc.
277 Broadway
New York, NY 10007

Library of Congress Cataloging-in-Publication Data
Nevison, Susannah, 1984–
[Poems. Selections]
Teratology : poems / Susannah Nevison.—First edition.
        pages cm
"A Karen & Michael Braziller Book."
Includes bibliographical references.
ISBN 978-0-89255-458-4 (original trade pbk. : alk. paper)
I. Title.
PS3614.E563T48 2015
811'.6—dc23
                        2014030283

First edition
Printed in the United States of America
Designed by Rita Lascaro

for my parents
and
for David

CONTENTS

I.

II.

III.

teratology [ˌtɛrəˈtɒlədʒɪ] *n.*

1. the branch of medical science concerned with the development of physical abnormalities during the fetal or early embryonic stage
2. the branch of biology that is concerned with the structure, development, etc., of monsters
3. a collection of tales about mythical or fantastic creatures, monsters, etc.

from Collins English Dictionary

I.

My Father Dreams of Horses

If your daughter is born
and her legs aren't made
for standing—if her feet
are painted hooves, if her legs
aren't made—if your daughter
is a wooden toy you dance

over a still field—if you must make
her limbs—if you carry her
to the river but the river
is made of horses—if you ride
into the forest—if flames—
if your daughter is made

like you, is built to burn—
if you wade into the horses—
if flames—if you cannot keep
her from burning—if she will not
keep—if the horses burn—
if your daughter is born—

Snow, Luminous

As if the snow
and all it tries to hide
weren't born of want too.

At the edge of the wood,
at the edge of one cold wound,
coyotes call their own.

Strange mouths wanting still,
a rabbit escapes beyond
teeth and endings.

Hunger like this feeds
on possibility. Your shadow
on snow is enough.

Preparing the Animal

I've been watching your hands
    for weeks, watching the rain gather
its woolen shawl around the house,
    while you sharpen tools, lay them out
and show me—*gut hook, drop point, skinner, priest*—
    what they can do, test each honed blade,
run the edge above your arm, close to skin,
    just close enough that tiny hairs bend or fall.
When I was a girl, a boy showed me a knife
    of steel I couldn't believe, though he insisted
it was real, dared me to touch it.
    I pressed my thumb to check its sharpness, certain
it was fake. I bled. The cut and sting
    fine as the stream of water

he then held my hand in, so cold
    it made me ache. What are we but sinew
and synapse, a system's grim accumulation,
    but softer? Soon, you will slit
the belly, you will enter with cupped hands
    to loose the windpipe and split
breastbone, the structure falling
    around the heart's muscled knot. I know
you will work quickly, not to staunch the wound
    but to bleed the body, to keep the meat, the hide,
will lay the body out, bless the knives—you, who cup my face
    gently, who drag your fingers
through my hair, until I bend
    or fall beside you.

Bestiary

As in all good stories, you walked
into the wolf's mouth and you were born:
when they found you, you had wrapped
yourself in the hide. You thought, *everyone forgets
the skin is the body's biggest organ.* You thought,
one heart can house another. And so you stood
in a body, and you called the body yours:
no one remembered your family. No one
had heard of your town. You walked
into the wolf's mouth and you were lost:
as in all good stories, they claimed
you for their own.

Lineage

I.

You with your surgeon's eye:
when the music and the promise
of cooler weather swelled
and caught in your throat
I helped you
harvest burled walnut.
We sought the mutant tangle,
a second sickness.
The whole orchard on its knees—

2.

In a ruined field, we cannot stop
watching the snowfall. We rend landscape
by hand, lose rows in the freeze.

We have already performed the burlap ritual, prepared
the trees to keep. Still, ice spreads like an accident.
We are hardened and cut like roads

and fields and rock: the burnt shoreline
of my father's scarred forearm. I watch him tend
the graft and wound, the sapling giving in his hands.

3.

    Last harvest season,
a mare knelt in the clearing, eyes unbridled—
    the slick crown emerging, mane wet and matted, a small
crooked marvel. Stillborn, his body a dark earthen mirror.
    Whisper *deformation* and listen: we razed the field,
we planted, we named—*bursa and bone*
    for the clenched limbs, finely muscled—

4.

The hunt for symmetry becomes one way
        of turning landscape into self,
assembling the greater picture, nature's

infinite repetition bleeding
        into a need for order, for answers—
which is to say, my skin is mapped

of my father's skin, the patterned sheen
        and stretch, that raised signature
of harm. In the light after the storm,

we moved among the trees, touched
        the damage, collected what was lost.
How else to reclaim one's body:

Fall into a ritual. Invent a course.
        I've seen whole orchards bloom from ash.

My Father Dreams of Horses

You told me you carried a stillborn
        foal to the river.
You told me the river didn't bless the body

but undressed its frame
        slowly, softening its handiwork.
That the ribs were licked

and how they shone, and how
        a ribcage hums in water.
You said sickness numbed the mare

like snow, weighing down
        her limbs. And sickness rocked
her body and sang

its off-key song, lulling her. You'd felt
        the swollen belly, the animal inside,
but everything you touched went still.

In another life, you carried me
        to the river: I was undone, a smear
of blood inking eddies in the water.

Lift me from the shoulders
        of the riverbank. See how ruin

carves our faces, how even my bones
        hold your name.

To Letheon

Where are you
leading me, cold cloud, cold
cloud? Who softens me
for gathering? Has the blade
become water—is it with water
they dress me, water they trail
over me—cold cloud, what
lightness do they spill?
What happens, what
happens when

    I wake—you

    wake—wake me—

Portrait as a Stand of Willows

When I enter the morning
    and give myself into the hands
of strangers, I need them to know me

    as the daughter of one struck branch,
dumb beneath the earth, still trading
    in my body for root and bloom.

I need to believe I've interred the lightning
    in my chest, that I am split with burning,
that I am brave as a river trading in

    what separates water from cutbank.
I am no one's mother. I have seen the men coming
    in distance, hauling their tools

on their backs. I have known
    for quite some time. The field gives
way. Men move among me. They take.

Genre Painting

This is where
the meat is tender
tracing the edge
of bone now,
tender here
and under
incarnadine fingers

of light reaching
across your face.
Your hand
does not flinch: knife
incandescent under
the hide, deep

under the body's
first remembrance—
head bent low,
the shadow of your face
kissing the blade.

II.

Lore

I.

They say you couldn't stop
singing. All night, the needle fed
you: stripped of most of your skin,
and the room around you white with metal
    refractions of light.

All night, someone stayed by the edge
of your bed, held the needle
in your ankle—the only place
fire hadn't claimed—held you
    while you kicked and sang.

2.

After he was burned, my father
        begged for more: he wanted the quiet
explosion in his blood—morphine, Demerol—
        he wanted numbness to wash his veins
of memory, the skeletal trees,
        his hands before him clutching
a can of gasoline. In his mind's dark,
        he could bend to earth, coax
the dry snap of a flame. He could steady
        his hands in time to stop
the can's woozy cough, the slow stain
        spreading down his shirt. He could imagine
it otherwise. But beyond himself, he sees
        himself go down, he still goes down
kicking among the burning trees.

3.

And night tightened its hold. And night
slipped its hands around my neck
and I did not cry out. Each planet burned
its name into the mirror of my eye,
flushing my skull with light: isn't this the way

I was born, the wide dark trembling, a swell
of blood pounding across distance,
forcing inlets between bone?
They say I was tied like a calf,
legs knotted for stumble. They say

I was a strange, mute animal.
Wild planets traced their circles
in my blood—my father beside me
trembling, my father steadying
his hands—the first star rising
where he cut the cord.

On the Discovery of a Feral Child

Gloves archive birthmark, blood type, bone,
      shine a light in your throat
and tug at your black tongue: neglect
      is doll and playmate, is guest,
and you carry dusk in your mouth.
      By turns brute and bird, you swell
your lungs with sound.

      Where
are your keepers now, the toothed and wild,
      who tore each season open
for you to feed on? You pressed your face
      between their flanks, grew
an appetite for heat—survival meaning
      hamstring or neck.

Under an eye that is not sun, there is no place
      now that does not teem with light.
Hush: they've come again to press
      a wooden horse into your chest.

Something Clinical

At what altar did you kneel, what cruel god
        pressed his thumb against your forehead and a stone
under your tongue and did not forgive. And still

the body knew, said *she is not mine*, its arched
        cavern breaking its own, twisting daughter legs into
daughter fins, a fish for a flower, cold reptilian

blue, sliding into first light: the murmurs *she is not
        right*, the feet tucked in and under, furled twins.
Coax her unfolded and plaster each limb, hold fast

 the binding but please show her how to survive
        this: force feet into molded shoes
and let her stand.

On the Surgical Dressing Change,
in Water, of a Five-Month-Old Child

To stop seeing her face
contort, skin recoil
from water's grip,

the fumble for the
end of gauze, scale-like
wrappings slip—toes

emerge now as seeds
unformed and pink
curled imperfections

this bent daughter
twisting in your hands:
three fingers of Jack

to quiet the mind's
echo, asking forgiveness
of you who held her

down in water, who
could not explain what
love asks us to endure—

who held her legs
tighter, to still the kick,
and would not let go.

To My Pre-Op Self as Marionette

I'll feed you
a line—*Maker, don't*
hesitate, just set that saw
to singing—so that he'll cut
your legs free from the linden
block, and stain them, too, all
while cradling your voice, faint as a child's
in the next room—and here, I'll feed you
another line—until you say *yes,*
to a name or *yes, please*
to his naming—and although you
are not his daughter you are born
by his hand, you answer
the name he cuts free in your mouth—
Molly and Cindy and Christy and Sam—
yes, you answer all the same—

Morphine, The Recurring Dream of Birds

That birds have bones
in their tongues—that they press
your hair in their beaks—that they carry

you home in pieces—your body
boneless as hair—that birds press
your bones in their beaks—that bodiless

hair lines a nest—that birds truss
their nest with your bones—that every
beak widens a wound—that birds

dive in, dive deep—that every wound
swallows a bird—that birds
dive straight to the bone—

that tendons are slender
as hair—that birds
tear muscle, tap bone—

that your bones ring hollow
as beaks—that birds carry
you home in pieces—

On the Physiology of the Heart

Recall the thin-skinned organ and visit the menagerie it houses:
elephant, loon, flora, hound. A clamor in the atrium. The animals have
hollowed out new passageways among their enclosures. You know the
structure, the folded and enfolded tunnels, has weakened. When you
release the animals, they know they should go, but tremble and remain.
Collapse is imminent. You threaten to whip the ones that stay, but
yoked to nothing their bodies assume helpless forms, and you can't
bring yourself to raise the switch. Instead, you kiss the heads of the
animals one by one. The heart collapses into river, into whitewater.
You open all the locks.

Post-Op Overdose

I was suture and gleam, a colony of mouths
      spitting metal. The lights were always on
and I was their celebrity: glinting

      in my cage, lacing the bars with gauze.
The gaudy baubles of trauma clustered
      about me, chirping and blinking,

pushing languid drams through
      their wires, patrolling my veins.
I showed you everything:

      how the deviant sprout persisted
in me, how the beasts guarded
      the thicket—and later, bloated

and terrible, how the beasts
      drifted for days. It's possible to love
what lays me to waste.

      The music of their bodies
in my latticed river dams—

Pre-Op Portrait with a Colony of Bats

They held the mask
        over your mouth, pumped you
full of forgetting: the sky
        fashioned a noose and hanged
herself, purpling and gasping—
        slackening, she let loose
her dusky children, shook them
        from their clustered lung of sleep,
spit them like broken teeth—their bodies
        swarmed your eyes, wings thin as any
eyelid—and you—you got it wrong—
        the owls never came—

Showroom

You dreamed that birds fell from the sky
     like paperweights, made of wire and stone.

They became an army of wind-up toys, drove
     their beaks into your legs, hunted worms.

When the surgical team stopped by your bed, you awoke
     but were barely lucid, and when you tried to tell them

you couldn't feel your leg, that you thought
     the fixator on your leg was made of wire beaks,

different words came out: *I'm afraid the birds will nest in me.*
     They removed the epidural and switched your meds.

They left you in the recovery room for seventeen hours
     because you grew to feel your leg too much

but couldn't move it, even though you tried to explain
     the birds were to blame. After seventeen hours, you realized

you'd have to lie. You'd have to say, *my pain is below a three
     on your scale.* After you were moved to a room,

the team came to unwind you. The first time you saw
     the fixator extending from your leg, bare,

you realized you'd underestimated thickness,
     that the pins weren't wire at all, but metal dowels,

that you weren't filled with birds, but with machinery.
     You were fascinated by your sudden complexity.

You were a radiant marionette. They gave you
     a schedule and a tool to manipulate your own device:

an L-wrench, the kind you'd use to assemble furniture.
     You began to dream of birds trapped inside couches,

of dead birds falling out of fold-out sofas,
     of expansive showroom floors. When the birds began

to resemble corduroy couches, you knew
     you'd had a breakthrough, that you were beginning

to understand. *I'm sorry that I lied about the pain.*
     Please show me how I work.

Experimentum Suitatis

'The organism is a unitary system,' but what
is a system to a real living self?
                              —Oliver Sacks

I.
Doubled-over body, wind-cut
        and burned, winnowed down
exactly twenty times to ragdoll
                and never   (or once) held—

                show me the spool
                        of your underbelly. Will you be left
                the finest skein of yourself,
                        and can I touch
                                you then— flow banded
                        veins, intricate maps running through—what
                                        marrow, what
                                belonging.

Take the fist out   of your mouth   Slow as a hardening stitch,
        this dripstone speech, porous   and thin-ringed.
        Tongue
            the rock salt and swallow: remember the stuff you are made.

Ribbon body opened   and exposed, fetters
            reflecting   every silver   filament.   There is
nowhere,   little one,
                    but deeper still: lose the flash
inside your   tender, hooked self.

2.

Fill the rafters
of your lungs, but carefully: what lives
and moves through you now, curling
into dark corners and out, brutal
        in its taking?
Make your mouth into the requisite
'O', let out the banshee. Outside
your window, birds
mark the day. Wait.

        What gathers
your breath for its own split song
returns your whittled
throat's dissonant notes—
your body an unhinged
        shell. Call it home.

To My Pre-Op Self as Etiological Myth

       And I am neither prophet
nor saint, but I was
       there when the ice calved
and you emerged, shouldering
       the dark mass of your body
into daylight, your twin
       limbs veined with lack
and fracture, the forceps an unasked
       oar ferrying you into the breach—
that sudden upswell and heave
       and all around you splitting.
I know the fault line
       in your blood before you, the infinite
wreck of bone, a tremor
       of history coursing through
with a pounding like so many hooves.
       Darkling, dear one, double:
believe me when I tell you it is written
       we should carry each other
until we break and split like the image
       in which we are made: the surgeon
a godhead who culls
       one weakness, yields another.

III.

Torsion

Each tendon's tender ribbon
pushed against the machine,
against metal pins mapping
the length of my leg—you work
my furious body, work my body
mean and loose—my body
humming metal—each pin a flag
in numbered, quartered land—
each pin a catch, a hitch that slows
the tendons' stretch—and each tendon
tightens, stops short, a horse
restive in its blinders resisting
the rider's urge and spur—your hands
the hands that hold the course,
that gentle and tender, loosen
and numb, drive headlong—
my body blind and dumb,
bridled or yoked, broken then
opened, run down into darkness,
run down—your hands
the hands that carry me—
and the machine's teeth
sink down, and the machine
hauls its gears—into my body's
wild and all its dangers—

Morphine, The Recurring Dream of Birds

In the slow hours, they touch me, hands I mistake for birds
threading nests with hair or swab or gauze. It isn't easy

to knit and suture just any old branded animal, each
sorrier than the next, so I do my best to bleed

cleanly, let the birds make a lesson of making me neat.
In the slowest hour, where they always find me.

What the Body Wants

To be adorned, to be gloved
in velvet earth, to be wanted—
to woo an audience of worms
with unrestrained carnality,
to let the lung cuss and burn,
to entice through its teeth
a smoldering lance—
to command a carnival
of crows, to prepare the feast—
to be the bride to your *yes,*
to your *more*—to say I do—
say don't—we all want
to be adored—

Ward

Collect me, name me, count me, make me, or so I'm saying
    to Rosa, or singing to Rosa, who is washing my back

and washing my hair, before the doctors come to deliver me
    news and instructions on maintenance and homecare

for the long haul—*I will be your happiest misfit toy,* or so I'm singing,
    forcing the words to the tune of Gilligan's Island

and mixing metaphors, and Rosa hums with me anyway,
    whispers, *you are my favorite patient, don't tell*—

and then leaves me alone so I might wash myself
    in private, I mean my privates, as if there is such a thing

as privacy in the half-curtained room I share with a woman
    named Effie, who calls the nurse every hour just on principle—

and I'm doing as Rosa has told me to do, just on principle,
    when the doctor rounds the curtain, and my hand

is clutching a sad washcloth, shoved in my crotch,
    which I can't even feel, and the doctor's embarrassed

and so he steps back—*excuse me,* he says, *excuse me.*
    Just tell me when you're decent.

Notes to the Body

I.

When you asked if I would stay with you, I wanted to say *yes, I'll always be your best girl.* I wanted to say, *everyone knows the body is a house and we're all carpenters here. You've got some serious home renovations going on.* It's summer and the kudzu is forcing its way up the trellis into every parted crevice. In a rocking chair on the front porch, I'm watching motherless flowers spread like water. I'd take you apart if I thought that would help. I'd take you apart myself.

2.

Don't say I've never done anything nice for you. I've never missed a tune-up. I've been thinking I should get us a subscription to one of those waiting-room mags. Feature: Relearning Body Basics 101. Feature: How to Get the Most Out of Your Relationship with Your Physical Therapist. Could we get a professional discount? I'm telling you, we've got to keep an eye out for some perks. Or start couponing. We could be good at that. We could start a collection. I've always wanted to be a collector.

3.

I didn't mean to bow out before the party started. How was the operating room? How were the cocktails? You came back pretty wrecked. I'm doing my best to get you what you need, keep you fed, hook you up with the good stuff. I'm doing my best not to leave. Sometimes I think one of us should get out more. Sometimes I think we're lonelier together.

4.

If they buried us, would someone find us with a metal detector? Where would you like to end up? I've always thought we might like a meadow. We'd look great in green. Or the sea: we would sink fast. We almost drowned once, off the coast of South Carolina. One of us crashed on the shore. The other drifted for days before she was found.

In the Long Grass Kneeling

The outermost skin of the trick: the vanished is
        still beholden to the body. What governs us

in departure, what releases. Tethered
        to return, lid-beats desperate against

the tower of your sleep, summon
        a face to look into for your own.

Instead, waking returns you, mind
        stripped down to riverbed. Ear turned toward water,

a coldness you understand: the deliberate grave you made
        yourself, a catch of leaves in each hipped bend

like a lingering sickness. You, too, are fond of pretending
        to be two people. Sooner or later, it's necessary

to reconcile what the eye sees
        with the image at hand—

lay the surface over the inked stone—
        river as given, river as blade.

Premortem

There's talk of *savage* or *salvage* or *salve*
and half-masked faces in your room.

They prepare to scrub the wild out, plunge your body
in cold light. The needle into the crook of your arm, an X
in paper tape to anchor it—they don't know

they've roused the hounds in your blood,
set the hounds running to open your throat
with their sleek, muscled heads, to snap

at the air, sound their note in your voice. It takes
a fleet of hands to force them down. A wooden tool
between your teeth. You are bathed in sweat.

You are bathed. Someone has turned down the bed
and someone is gentle. Your hair has been cut
and now combed, and combed again. The dogs

curl tightly in the heart's dark chamber, folding
into sleep. They dream of surrender, of laying their bodies
down into earth. Into their country

you follow. Elsewhere, someone runs a dull blade
beneath your nails to bring out the dirt.

My Father Dreams of Horses

The barn caught
the barn went up
your horse got loose

snorting and stamping
your horse caught
by the fence the fire

caught your horse
ran loose into the night
the edge of the forest

bled horses the trees
streamed with horses
the trees caught

you couldn't catch
your horse the trees
caught you went down

but you never had a horse
never the horse burned
never the barn

Look How Dark the Mountain Is

Made of rock pressed into itself,
pushed northward, a hard turn toward
sky, what the earth allowed when plates
vied for space. And the earth was made
of bodies pressed into themselves, blood
rusted into soil, a hard turn of luck.
We murdered the livestock.
       We took down every living thing.

You with a shotgun. Me with poison.
We numbered the deaths on trees,
watched the pyre smoke curl and blacken
and we said it was perfect, said it was a gift
to be divested of light, to be cut to the quick.
Take the flies: already they are blooming
       terrible flowers out of the animals' eyes.

For Whom Grief

I mean to say how he worked the rows for hours,
hoe steady in his hand, striking earth again and again—

how we watched night settle
as he leaned against the hoe,
wiping his brow with the back of his arm,

and then, wielding his instrument,
began again—
how we quietly left a plate out—

mornings, plate scraped clean
and he, in the distance, at it again—

Another Kind of Clay

I enter my own house quietly
        and another board gives out.
A coat hangs slack on its nail,

a wanting husk, how the abandoned
        return as ash and scatter.
Because grief is both root

and transport, transient silt,
        I touch each careful object
for a glint of history, another

kind of clay. We can spend our whole lives
        trying to inhabit our lives.

The dogged bondstone holds. Someone
        sings. Is singing.

Event Horizon

It was October or it was Ohio,
you, long-legged, moved
as a horse over field.

Wild and skinned, kneeling
or head bent. You offered up
the raw, raked-down.

Call this into focus, this length
of river: it was only the mouth,
and it was endless.

Marshland

I mean last winter—
an illness settled in and wind
keened at the windows, licking
the glass. What the wind took:
      milkweed, nettles, twigs. All the leaves

she could carry. Then snow stretched
across the ice like a sterile bedsheet.
What it looks like to be leveled: each wound
a yawn stopped with cotton.
I watched the wind bend
      what she'd left behind.

When spring came, the river drew
the headwaters like a syringe, sucking
the marsh dry. What the river took:
      what the wind didn't want.

Open My Body

and let a river in me
startle my heart's pool
let my blood
flush the starlings
from its stark forest of bone
and enter the rough country
kneel down in the waters
where an animal crouches
snow-flecked and lithe
lowering its head to drink
trouble the gleaming surface
where nothing holds

If You Come to the Sea and You Must Cross

And you have nothing to offer,
or there's no lighthouse winking
to keep your hands on course.

You know light does not fracture
all things equally. And so you
try your hand at sharpness

without hesitation, even though
you cannot see where your knife
might land, even though

you cannot see that a length
of driftwood is your own
bare leg. You build

with rotted wood, or limb,
or bone: you turn
into vessel, into hollow,

so that you might enter the sea
wanting, your cheek lined
with salt. Water opens its skin

to accept what you will give.
When the good work is done
           you begin.

NOTES

"To Letheon" derives its title from the first form of inhalation anesthesia, commonly known as sulphuric ether. In Boston in 1846, dentist William T. G. Morton famously demonstrated ether's use as an anesthetic agent, but tried to mask the identity of the drug, and later tried to patent it, by using the term "letheon" to refer to the substance.

"Experimentum Suitatis" borrows its epigraph from Oliver Sacks's book *A Leg To Stand On.*

"For Whom Grief" borrows its title from a line from Rainer Maria Rilke's "Duino Elegies" ("First Elegy," translated by Stephen Mitchell): *"But we, who do need / such great mysteries, we for whom grief is so often / the source of our spirit's growth—"*

"Look How Dark the Mountain Is" is for SEJ.

ACKNOWLEDGEMENTS

I am grateful to the editors and staff at the following publications, in which some of these poems first appeared, sometimes in different forms or under different titles:

American Literary Review: "Preparing the Animal"
Cider Press Review: "Lore"; "Something Clinical"
Diode Poetry Journal: "Open My Body"; "Marshland"
The Journal: "Premortem"
New Orleans Review: "Another Kind of Clay"; "In the Long Grass Kneeling"; "Look How Dark the Mountain Is"
New Southerner: "For Whom Grief"
Ninth Letter: "My Father Dreams of Horses"; "My Father Dreams of Horses (II)"
Southern Indiana Review: "To My Pre-Op Self as Marionette"; "To My Pre-Op Self as Etiological Myth"; "If You Come to the Sea and You Must Cross"; "Portrait as a Stand of Willows"; "Notes to the Body"
Sycamore Review: "My Father Dreams of Horses (III)"
The The Poetry Blog: "Bestiary"; "Morphine, The Recurring Dream of Birds (I)"; "On the Physiology of the Heart"
Western Humanities Review: "Genre Painting"

"Preparing the Animal" was selected by Alan Michael Parker for the 2013 *American Literary Review* poetry prize.

"My Father Dreams of Horses (I)" was selected by Ilya Kaminksy for a 2013 Academy of American Poets/Larry Levis prize.

"If You Come to the Sea and You Must Cross" received the 2014 Patricia Aakhus award from *Southern Indiana Review.*

Many thanks to the Taft-Nicholson Center and the Dee Foundation for providing funding, time, and space to work on these poems, and to the Lexi Rudnitsky Poetry Project and Persea Books for selecting this manuscript and ushering it into the world. Special thanks to my editor, Gabriel Fried, for his keen insight and support.

My most heartfelt gratitude to my teachers, colleagues, and students at the University of Southern California, Columbia University, and the University of Utah, especially Molly Bendall, Lucie Brock-Broido, Katharine Coles, Timothy Donnelly, Eamon Grennan, Richard Howard, David St. John, Jacqueline Osherow, and Paisley Rekdal. Without your patience, guidance, and generosity, this book wouldn't exist.

For their unwavering support and belief in my work, I am indebted to Laura Bylenok, Meg Day, Sara Eliza Johnson, Christopher Kondrich, Christina LaPrease, Michael Simon, and Claire Wahmanholm. Immeasurable love and gratitude to my parents, Jack and Nancy; to Laura, Vince, and Lucia; and to Mary, Larry, Danny, and Shaun. Above all, thanks to my husband, David, for weathering the storm with love, humor, and grace.